BRITAIN
THE FIRST COLOUR PHOTOGRAPHS

BRITAIN
THE FIRST COLOUR PHOTOGRAPHS
Images of Wartime Britain

ROGER A. FREEMAN

CHANCELLOR
PRESS

Left: Piccadilly Circus at 22 minutes past two on a sunny afternoon in 1944. The famous statue of Eros was removed and its plinth sandbagged in the early days of the war. Later it was boarded up and used to display savings posters while the buildings bordering the entrance to Shaftesbury Avenue still flaunted their once illuminated pre-war advertisements for alcohol, beverages, cigarettes and chewing-gum. (Cal Sloan)

Acknowledgments
The colour photographs in this book are reproduced through
the kindness of the men who took them half a century ago.
They are, in alphabetical order: Robert Astrella, Eugene Blue,
Mark Brown, Tom Cooper, Arnold Delmonico, Jack Havener,
Milton Holley, Albert Krassman, Edmund Lutz, Robert Malster, John Meyers, George Parker, John Phegley, Herb Rutland, Robert Sand, Alexander 'Cal' Sloan, Byron Trent and
Stan Wyglendowski. Owing to the effect of the passage of
time on the usual human notion that one will have no diffi-
culty in remembering where and when a photograph was
taken, in many cases the veterans cannot now recall the
locations for several of their photographs. To overcome this,
the compiler enlisted the help of the following individuals in
Britain who were able to make positive identifications of subjects depicted or supplied details: Andrew Anderson, Carol
Aitkin, John W. Archer, John Bridges, David Crow, Phyllis
DuBois, Simon Forty, John Greenwood, Paul Kemp, Robert
Kuhnert, Robert Malster, Norman McGrail, D. P. Dam Mort-
lock, Norman R. Ottaway, George Pennick, Ann Richards,
Ronald Sismey, Lorna Smerden, Ella Thurmott, Dr Peter War-
dle, Paul and Hilary Warburton and Dr Jonathan Wright.
Clarence House, the Imperial War Museum, the ladies of
Oxford's Historic Photographic Archive, Essex and Norfolk
County Libraries also provided much appreciated assistance.
Particular thanks are due to Bruce Robertson for his extensive knowledge and use of his records on the wartime scene
in Britain; additionally, his editorial advice. Special thanks
are also due to Ian Mactaggart for his skill in the necessary
photographic processing work involved in this project. Jean
Freeman and the faithful Alice Apricot provided the final
copy. All of the above, in greater or lesser degrees, played a
part in making this publication possible and it is hoped that
they find it worthy of their efforts. To all I offer my sincere
thanks.

Roger A. Freeman, Dedham, England.

Right: For a wartime young-
ster, having your picture
taken was an event, but this
lad probably had no idea
that his pose in a west Suffolk village street would be
in rare colour. (Mark Brown)

CONTENTS

INTRODUCTION

This book contains reproductions of some of the first colour photographs ever taken of the subjects – and in many cases undoubtedly the first. There is a natural human tendency for each generation to accept without question or wonder the technological developments commonplace in their formative years. Many things taken for granted now were once unknown and, perhaps, uncommon to the previous generation. Such can be said of colour photography, the normal form in the late twentieth century, but it was exceptionally rare until after the Second World War. The British public's introduction was through colour reproductions on the covers of popular magazines, where the high cost could be commercially justified. When the film stock became generally available in the post-war years, colour transparencies in the form of slides were a novelty. Colour prints did not become generally available until the Sixties.

Although various techniques for colour photography had been devised in the early years of the century, it was not until 1935, when Kodak introduced Kodachrome, that a reliable and commercially viable process was marketed in the USA. In transparency form it was immediately taken up by the motion picture industry and the 'still' market took some time to develop because of cost and the fact that the images were not readily seen, the transparency slides having to be projected or used in a magnifying viewer. Little of this still stock reached Britain because initially the processing of Kodachrome was only carried out in the USA. When local facilities did become available on a limited scale in 1939, the importation of the film stock ceased with the outbreak of war. A process known as Dufaycolour was used by some British photographers in the late Thirties. While more affordable than Kodachrome, it was generally held to be less colour true and reliable.

Apart from one or two professional news photographers with American contacts and British government agencies, Kodachrome stock was not available to the British public during the Second World War. For that matter, very little monochrome film could be purchased by amateurs after 1942. By the time the United States entered hostilities at the end of 1941, Kodachrome slides were gaining in popularity with that nation. Despite regulations forbidding the use of private cameras on military installations, it appears that a great many US servicemen brought their Kodak Bantam, Argos, and other popular makes, plus a few Kodak Ektra which was specially marketed for use with Kodachrome film.

On leave, the American servicemen visited places they had learned about at school or in the British classics and magazines. Their cameras went too and recorded what might be called the traditional tourist trail: Tower of London, St Paul's Cathedral, Stratford-upon-Avon, the Lake District, Edinburgh Castle, the Highlands and the rest. The GI (the generic term used for all US military personnel by the British) was also drawn to photograph that which was unlike anything he had ever seen back home, either because it was ancient or just plain different. Ruined castles, country mansions, centuries old churches, thatched cottages, 'dinky autos' and 'railroad locos' were popular among his broad range of subjects. Many American servicemen took full advantage of the opportunity afforded to explore this country, steeped in history and from whose colonial enterprise their own great nation had sprung. Their exploratory interest belies the popular legend of the pub-crawling, girl-chasing GI.

Of several who took colour photographs, there were probably only about a half dozen true enthusiasts who ranged far and wide in the United Kingdom shooting Kodachrome. The majority of these wartime visitors kept to conventional monochrome film. Three enlisted men, Robert Astrella, Robert Sand and Alexander Cal Sloan were the principal colour enthusiasts whose work is featured in this book. All three amassed sizeable collections during their time in Britain and preserved them during the following years. Considering the limitations of the cameras available and used, their work was outstanding. This is not to depreciate the work of other US military personnel whose photographs appear on the following pages, for while their use of colour was not so extensive and they did not range so far or so often, they produced many excellent pictures. The majority of the reproductions cover the later war years, 1943 to 1945, reflecting the peak period of the friendly American invasion of wartime Britain.

Bringing this material together here, produces what is perhaps the earliest wide-ranging photographic survey of Britain in colour. The compiler can find no comparable collection in published form that pre-dates these wartime pictures. And while they are of domestic, rural, architectural and historical subjects, many contain some indication of the time showing that what is depicted is wartime Britain in colour.

Right: In his famous book *Three Men in a Boat,* an idyllic outing on the Thames, Jerome K. Jerome wrote of the Barley Mow Inn, near Clifton Hamden, Oxfordshire: 'It is without exception I should say the quaintest most old-world inn up the river' Dating from 1352, part of the building was severely damaged by fire post Second World War. (Robert Astrella)

THE METROPOLIS

The world's most well-known city, then the hub of an empire and the Western Allies' chief nerve centre of the conflict with Adolf Hitler's regime, London did not lack for visitors during the years 1939 to 1945, although most were military personnel drawn from many nations. Despite the danger of air raids, London still attracted sightseers among the leave-takers.

By the time the camera-toting GI arrived on the scene the Blitz was history and while the Luftwaffe did not neglect this city, the attacks were occasional and far removed from the 76 consecutive nights of bombardment suffered during the winter of 1940–41. Even the V-1 flying-bomb deluge in the summer of 1944 and the V-2 rocket assault that followed did little to deter US service personnel. There were eventually fifteen American Red Cross hostels in central London alone, specially set up to afford accommodation and recreational facilities for these men and women on two- or three-day passes. The available entertainments were an attraction, but a great many of these North American visitors sought out

Left: The Royal Standard flies over Buckingham Palace indicating that the Sovereign is in residence. The passing fire services lorry and the white painted road kerbs mark the scene as wartime. The palace was bombed in September 1940; damage sustained, which was mainly to precincts, included the private chapel, swimming-bath and pavilions. (Cal Sloan)

historic institutions and places famed even in their homeland.

At weekends during 1944 and early 1945 there did not appear to be a street in central London without an ambling GI. Interestingly, most did not contravene the decree that there should be no unofficial photography of damage caused by recent enemy action. Even so, only one building in ten in central London did not sustain some form of damage and it is remarkable that with the exception of the area around St Paul's there are so few signs of damage in the following selection of photographs.

Above: The crowd applauded when Queen Mary, the then Queen Mother, emerged from jewellers, Cameo Corner, Holborn, to return to her Daimler on 3 July 1945. (Robert Sand)

Right: A team of horses used for royal occasions seen out on exercise near The Mall. (Cal Sloan)

Above: A statesman looks down from his pedestal on the Embankment as a lorry and taxicab pass Big Ben. The repair to the tower where a bomb (fortunately a dud) struck the upper right-hand corner, can be seen above the clock. The recorded chimes of Big Ben were broadcast world-wide throughout the war as a preface to selected daily news bulletins as a symbol to the occupied countries of Europe that Britain was continuing the struggle. (Cal Sloan)

Top left: 'Didn't expect to see this guy here': GIs find a statue of their sixteenth President, Abraham Lincoln, in Westminster, spring 1944. (Cal Sloan)

Bottom left: Sergeant Joe Harris, a Mormon, with a PhD in chemistry, poses with a police sergeant against a background of the Thames, Westminster Abbey and the Houses of Parliament (with the inevitable scaffolding). The London bobby was far removed from the US cop in both uniform and behaviour. (Cal Sloan)

Right: During 1940 the stained glass window of the west front of Westminster Abbey was removed and stored elsewhere to avoid bomb blast. Hit by incendiaries on the night of 10/11 May 1941, the roof of the Abbey was damaged but the fire was contained through early warning from Fire Watchers. (Cal Sloan)

Left: The launch of 'Salute The Soldier' week on Saturday 25 March 1944 in Trafalgar Square. Opened by Field Marshal Sir Alan Brooke, Chief of the Imperial General Staff, it was linked to one of the many government sponsored saving drives, the target being £165,000,000. A view towards The Strand with South Africa House on the far left. The uniforms of many Allied services are visible – and not a pigeon in sight! (Cal Sloan)

Right: The Lord Mayor of London, Sir Frank Newson-Smith, arrives to visit the 'Salute The Soldier' exhibition in Trafalgar Square. Born in 1879, Sir Frank Newson-Smith was a stockbroker and member of the London Stock Exchange. The white painted mudguard rim of his car was a blackout aid. The National Gallery is in the background. (Cal Sloan)

Left: Most GIs who visited London made for the most famous of all American Red Cross Clubs, Rainbow Corner. Next to the old Monico Restaurant in Shaftesbury Avenue on the corner of Great Windmill Street, it could cater for up to 2,000 servicemen at a time, providing accommodation, entertainment and refreshments. It was frequently visited by celebrities and had a staff of more than 300. (Cal Sloan)

Left:. Lower Regent Street, heart of the West End, on a rainy day in the spring of 1945, with a horse-drawn delivery van and Austin and Wolseley cars. Many Americans were left with the impression that England was extraordinarily wet. While the maritime climate produces many damp days, average rainfall in the London area is in fact only 21 inches per annum. (Byron Trent)

Right: A guard party near Clarence House led by a kilted pipe band. Such details brightened the everyday scene in wartime London. (Byron Trent)

Right: The Albert Memorial on Easter Sunday 1944, viewed from Kensington Gardens. Civilian and military strollers make for Hyde Park to enjoy the promise of spring. A relic of Victorian grandeur, the Memorial represents the Queen's mourning for her consort. It took ten years to complete and cost the then vast sum of £120,000. A 175-foot-high dome covers the bronze of Prince Albert, but the most noteworthy feature is the frieze with sculptured portraits of practitioners of the Arts. It did not go unnoticed by one GI that there was not 'a single dame' among the 178 figures. (Cal Sloan)

Above: The war did not lessen the activities of the political and religious zealots at Speakers' Corner, Hyde Park. A range of ages in military and civilian garb (including a Royal Marine) were attracted to this man with the Good Book on a spring Sunday in 1944. (Cal Sloan)

Left: St Paul's from Cheapside with bombed buildings on the right. Shrapnel scars can be seen on the cathedral, which was damaged on several occasions and threatened by an unexploded bomb which was defused. The most serious damage was sustained on 16 April 1941 when a bomb penetrated the North Transept and exploded on the floor. (Cal Sloan)

Left: The Royal Courts of Justice, more commonly known as the Law Courts, at the eastern end of The Strand. Built between 1866 and 1882, the building sustained damage from a V-1 flying-bomb in 1944, a few days after this photograph was taken. (Cal Sloan)

Below: The rooftops around Ludgate Circus and Fleet Street, seen from St Paul's on an afternoon in 1944. (Cal Sloan)

Below: Another view from the dome of St Paul's showing the cleared bombsites on each side of Cannon Street. The shattered arching roof of Cannon Street Station, seen on the right, was so badly damaged that it was dismantled. Pointing above the skyline, centre, is the 202-foot-high Monument column designed by Christopher Wren and erected in 1677 to commemorate the Great Fire of London which started in its vicinity. (Cal Sloan)

Right: St Mary-le-Bow, Cheapside, which was partially destroyed by bombs on the night of 10 May 1941. One of London's most ancient churches, part of the old London Wall c. 1080 was incorporated into its crypt. The steeple, rebuilt by Christopher Wren 1670-83 after the Great Fire of London, survived the Blitz. This is the church of Bow Bells, of which it is said that a true cockney is one born within earshot of their sound. Photographed during the time of the V-2 attacks, 18 December 1944. (Robert Sand)

Left: Fleet Street, home of the nation's press, with plenty of office space to let on this damp morning of 12 October 1944. London was in the midst of Hitler's V-weapon campaign. After the 1940-41 Blitz many businesses that had moved out of London gradually returned, then the V-1 and V-2 bombardment gave rise to another spate of 'To Let' notices throughout the City. (Robert Sand)

Above: Billingsgate porters and a London bobby (who wears medal ribbons for First World War service) at the famous fish market, 24 July 1944. The newspaper headlines read: 'Night and Day Air Onslaught'. (Robert Sand)

Left: A tug with a pair of partly loaded lighters heads upstream towards Tower Bridge. Built for the City Corporation in 1886-94, the bridge cost £1,500,000. (Cal Sloan)

Top right: The bascules of Tower Bridge raised to let a sailing barge pass upstream. It took only a minute and a half for the bascules to be fully raised. The vessel on the right, painted in two shades of grey as camouflage, belongs to the General Steam Navigation Company, the world's oldest shipping line, founded in 1824. (Cal Sloan)

Bottom right: Tower Bridge traffic, April 1944. The White Tower can be seen in the background. (Cal Sloan)

Left: The Tower of London from Tower Hill looking south-east on a spring afternoon in 1944. More than 900 years old and chiefly used as a royal prison, the Tower is a major London museum but in wartime most of its most precious holdings, such as the crown jewels, were removed to safety. (Jack Havener)

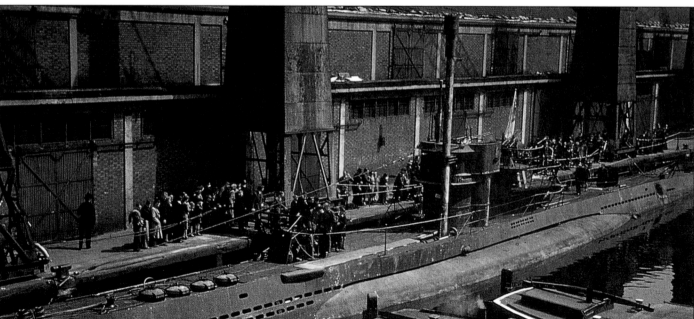

Left: People queuing to board the surrendered *U-776* in London Docks in May 1945. After display at other locations, this U-boat was finally sunk in deep water in the Atlantic. (Cal Sloan)

THE GREAT UNIVERSITIES

As seats of academic excellence, the Universities of Oxford and Cambridge had a pre-war reputation second to none. Both towns, as they were at the time, drew many American servicemen, particularly Cambridge which was in the centre of the main area of US Army Air Forces airfields. Oxford was on the periphery but still had its full share of American visitors, yet was probably better known to them from the 1938 Robert Taylor film, *A Yank At Oxford*. At both places the principal attractions were the many ancient colleges, buildings

Right: The largest and most majestic of all the Oxford Colleges, Christ Church, is dominated by its Tom Tower, named after Great Tom, the bell cast in 1680 and housed therein. The bell, weighing six tons, rings 101 times at 9.05 every evening. This was originally the curfew call that the college gates would be shut and barred. When this photograph was taken it had not rung since 1940. The ringing of bells in wartime was restricted to an invasion warning only. (Robert Astrella)

which had in many cases stood for several centuries before the United States came into being. The medieval collegiate system, with its equally old orders and ceremonies, also intrigued those from the newer, less traditionally endowed, higher educational academies of the New World.

While both Oxford and Cambridge attracted comparatively little attention from the Luftwaffe and the ancient buildings were more troubled by a period of maintenance neglect than by enemy ordnance, these seats of learning were inevitably disrupted by the war. The tutorial staff numbers were eventually down to two-thirds of the pre-war total, but while the overall numbers of students fell by more than a quarter, these were predominantly male as the numbers of women actually rose. Even so, much of the scholarly activity was directed to causes that could help the war effort. While Oxford and Cambridge suffered few significant air raids, both towns had war industries, particularly Oxford, whose important motor industry was heavily into fighting vehicles.

The off-duty GI drawn to Oxford and Cambridge also indulged in the favourite activity of the college students described as 'messing about on the river'. Commercial facilities for oar-, paddle- or pole-propelled boats of various kinds were maintained on both the Thames and the Cam throughout the war.

Left: Posing before the Mercury fountain in Tom Quad at Christ Church, a picture for the folk back home. In 1941 the college building served as a clearing house for refugee families from the London Blitz when babies' nappies were strung out on makeshift linen lines in Tom Quad. (Robert Astrella)

Right: Christ Church Cathedral, the ancient monastic college church, as seen from Merton Fields. The spire is probably the oldest in England, dating from the thirteenth century. (Robert Astrella)

Left: Broad Street, Oxford, spring 1945 with No 51, Blackwells, one of the most famous bookshops in England, which began in one room in 1879. Further down the street on the right is Trinity College (founded 1554) and at the far end Balliol (founded *c.*1263). (Robert Astrella)

Right: Salters boatyard provided steamboat cruises on the Thames even in wartime. The yard was west of Folly Bridge, a name derived from the quaint houses in the vicinity, not the bridge which is conventional and is on the south approach to Inner Oxford and is believed to be at the point of the original ford from which the city's name is derived. The vessels in the photograph, *Reading* and *Iffley,* carried many thousands of sightseers during their 30 years' service. (Robert Astrella)

Right: An ornate college barge owned by Talboys & Son on the Thames at Oxford, May 1945. In later ownership this vessel served for parties and conventions moored at Goring on Thames, where it was still to be seen 50 years after this photograph was taken. (Robert Astrella)

Left: College barges for watching water sports moored on the Thames at Oxford. A view towards Folly Bridge with Christ Church Meadow on the right bank. (Robert Astrella)

Below: Looking up King's Parade, Cambridge, with the entrance to the First court of King's College on the left, and the famous chapel beyond, which partly obscures the Old Schools, the University administration centre. Unlike the railings of the Cambridge householders whose garden and house railings were compulsory taken for scrap metal during the war years, the railings of the Senate House, on the right, remained undisturbed as they had since 1730, a point of contention between Town and University at the time. (Cal Sloan)

Above: The Master's Lodge of Christ's College, Cambridge, viewed across the beautifully manicured lawn of the First Court. There was no fuel for motor mowers in wartime and such maintenance had to be done with push lawn mowers and considerable effort. (Cal Sloan)

Left: Boys of the world famous King's College Chapel choir in their Eton suits draw the attention of a British Army private as they cross King's Bridge with a tutor on route from chapel to school. Across the lawns is the Fellows' Building of King's, built 1724, the work of architect James Gibbs. (Cal Sloan)

Right: King's College Chapel. This famous building is one of to be the few medieval churches that has retained its original stained glass. Here the windows are protected by heavy screening to keep them safe from bomb blast. (Mark Brown)

Right: Many a GI stood in awe before these panelled doors that have hung there since 1515, more than a century before the Pilgrim Fathers set foot in North America. St John's College Gate Tower with the statue of the saint and its ornate display has few equals. The emblems of Lady Margaret Beaufort, college benefactress and mother of King Henry VII, embellish the statue, below which are yales (mythical antelope-like creatures with the facility for moving horns independently) supporting the Lancastrian Arms. As the sign indicates, the tower was used by fire watchers as a section point. The fire watchers were usually members or employees of the College, identified by yellow armbands with the words 'Fire Guard' when on duty. Their normal equipment was a hand-operated stirrup pump, sandbags and sand-filled buckets for dealing with incendiary bombs, but their chief responsibility was reporting fires to the National Fire Service during air raids. (Robert Astrella)

Right: The Great Gate from the other side has statues of King James I, his wife Anne and son Charles, identifying the royal patronage. A view across Trinity College, Great Court which is the largest court of any college. The canopied fountain was built in 1610 and was supplied with water from springs a mile away. Even in wartime, gowns were worn by college members. In fact the two Cambridge authorities of Town and University were known as town and gown. (Cal Sloan)

Above: St John's College, so-called New Court with cloister walk at the front, looking across The Backs over well-kept lawns. (Cal Sloan)

Right: The Great Gate entrance to Trinity College, erected between 1528 and 1535. A statue of King Henry VIII, the College's founder, was added nearly a century later. During the war years, as now, there were cycle racks but no longer is it mandatory, as it was then, to have six inches of the rear mudguard painted white. (Cal Sloan)

Left: The east range of the Old Schools, 1757-58, based on London's Horse Guards. (Cal Sloan)

Right: Enjoying hire boats on the River Cam at the back of St John's College. Two girls in a punt, two boys in a canoe and against the bank a rob-roy. Their clothes would mark this picture as from the nineteen-forties without the US serviceman his WAAF girl-friend and other uniformed individuals on the banks. (Cal Sloan)

Right: GIs try out a canoe while British servicemen cycle over King's Bridge. Looking towards Clare, the oldest bridge over the Cam with Scholar's Piece on the left; April 1944. (Cal Sloan)

Left: Spring sunshine on The Backs at King's College. A good place for boy to meet girl and girl to meet boy, although on this Sunday afternoon the fair sex predominates. To the left is Clare College, founded 1326. (Cal Sloan)

Above: The so-called Market Hill with a Saturday flower stall to brighten the scene. Looking north towards Market Street and Mackintosh the ironmongers. The typical small British lorries of the time had a 2-ton load capacity. (Mark Brown)

Left: Bicycles, a twentieth-century feature of Cambridge streets, were the predominant personal transport in the nineteen-forties. This is Trinity Street from the King's Parade end, with confectioners Matthews & Sons on the left and the Blue Boar Hotel farther down. The Morris saloon is registered for US use as a staff car. (George Parker)

Left: The former Bull Hotel was one of the largest enlisted men's American Red Cross Clubs in Cambridge. It was situated in King's Parade and nearly opposite Corpus Christi College. (Cal Sloan)

Right: The Church of the Holy Sepulchre, dating from the early twelfth century, in Bridge Street, Cambridge, was a particular curiosity to US airmen because it was round, one of only five so shaped in England. The building at the right is Marshall's Garage. The proprietor opened a flying-school pre-war which was in use by the RAF for elementary flying training when this photograph was taken on a Sunday afternoon in the spring of 1945. (Mark Brown)

Left: The Lent Races on the Cam where college racing eights compete to overtake the boat in front and so record a 'Bump' to move up the league table, the top eight having the title Head of the River. Coaches on bicycles ride along the tow-path calling the stroke through megaphones. These races were held downstream where the river was wider, in the Chesterton area. (Cal Sloan)

Left: The strange English game called cricket and its all-white uniform – although one player has not sacrificed his precious clothing coupons on white trousers. The batsman is about to meet the ball in this game on the Cambridge playing fields off Barton Road in the summer of 1944. (Cal Sloan)

THE TOURIST TRAIL

Few United States citizens could afford to visit Europe prior to the Second World War, either because of the cost or the time to make the trans-Atlantic sea journey. As a result, there was not much in the way of a tourist industry in the United Kingdom where visitors from such far-off lands were concerned. Nevertheless, many well-read and informed Americans knew of places worth seeing. Those recruited into the US services and sent to Britain during the war years became the pioneers of the so-called tourist trails that millions of their country folk would take in the second half of this century. At that time it required a fair degree of determination, for travel in wartime Britain was not easy. With all private motoring, apart from 'essential' uses banned from mid-war, an extra strain was put on public transport. Buses and trains were usually filled to capacity and subject to delay and cancellation for a variety of reasons.

Right: Windsor, a royal castle since Norman times, with the main drive through the Great Park. Only the barbed wire roadblock, just visible on the right of the picture, gives a clue to the period. (Robert Astrella)

A 48-hour pass did not give much time for travelling far for the majority of US service personnel, who were based in the south-eastern quarter of England. The real enthusiasts allowed their leave time to mount up so that, with a longer period available, they could venture farther afield. Even so, there were some famed locations they were unable to reach or just could not find in a land devoid of place name signs and directional indicators throughout most of the war years. One GI who idolized Robin Hood made three unsuccessful attempts to find Sherwood Forest, despite helpful directions from Nottingham natives. But then Sherwood Forest was not quite what it might seem to those who knew only of the legend. Many Americans were primed on what to see and where to visit by British friends and acquaintances, although if the place were landscape it often tended to disappoint men raised within sight of some of the spectacular lake and mountain scenery of North America.

Above: Looking through the entrance gates at Windsor Castle, the photographer also caught a familiar sight of 1944, a formation of Flying Fortresses returning from a bombing raid. (Robert Astrella)

Left: The main gate of Windsor Castle on the afternoon of 24 August 1944. This was built for Henry VIII, one of the many monarchs who added to the work of William the Conqueror over some 900 years of the castle's existence. (Robert Sand

Above: A considerable crowd was watching this lady exercise her dog on the lawn before Windsor Castle's Henry III Tower (left) and the Round Tower of Edward III, on Thursday, 24 August 1944. Royalty or a scullery maid? (Robert Sand)

Above right: The Long Mile, Windsor Great Park, which runs to 1,800 acres, seen on 24 August 1944. The double row of fine elms fell victim to Dutch Elm Disease in post-war years. The three-mile drive was created for Charles II in 1685. (Robert Sand)

Right: The Bard's home town. A main street at Stratford-upon-Avon at the junction with Ely Street, in the spring of 1944. Apart from the shelter sign, the water pipe laid beside the kerb for fire fighting is a sign of wartime. (Jack Havener)

Left: Probably the most photographed thatch in England, Anne Hathaway's so-called cottage, but was this the first in colour? Located at Shottery, a mile from the centre of Stratford-upon-Avon, it was restored by the Trustees of Shakespeare's Birthplace in 1892. (Robert Astrella)

Right: The fifteenth-century bridge over the Avon with the Shakespeare Memorial Theatre beyond. This building was completed in 1932 after an earlier structure burned down in 1926. (Robert Astrella)

Left: Canterbury's East Gate. The steel pipe scaffolding was part of the anti-invasion defences. The small boys in the picture were no doubt about to approach the photographer for gum. (Jack Havener)

Right: Looking towards the altar and Trinity Chapel in Canterbury Cathedral, 7 February 1945, Robert Sand was so busy setting up his camera that he was unaware he had been locked in. 'A very spooky place in the deepening gloom and the air reeks with history,' he recorded in his diary. Fortunately an attendant returned that evening, something he rarely did, and found the prisoner. (Robert Sand)

Right: The incongruous presence of concrete tank obstacles before the eastern wall of Canterbury Cathedral. These were intended to halt the passage of tanks, the irony in this case being that Canterbury had been given a First World War tank as a war trophy which was installed in the Cathedral grounds but eventually went for scrap. The Cathedral was badly shaken on the night of 31 May 1942 when bombs damaged buildings in the precincts, but only the library was completely destroyed. (Jack Havener)

Left: The narrow North Gate, Canterbury, with black-and-white blackout markers. Photographed on 7 February 1945 when it was in use as a police station. (Robert Sand)

Right: The famous Pulteney Bridge in Bath, commissioned by William Pulteney in 1770 and built four years later by Robert Adam. Pulteney's further projects were temporarily thwarted by the government buying up all building supplies for the American War of Independence! The bridge links Bridge Street with Argyle Street, the photograph being taken from the weir looking upstream on the Avon. (Cal Sloan)

Left: The font of a hot spring in the Royal Baths, dating back to Roman times, which was in use in baths up to 1939 – although the colour of the water was not conducive to bathing. In the various reconstructions of post-war years this font's position was submerged. The baths and Assembly Room area were among 200 buildings of historical interest in Bath that received damage during air raids. (Cal Sloan)

Right: Late thirteenth-century Valley Farm, Flatford, Suffolk; the home of the Lott family in John Constable's day and to be seen in one of his paintings. The house is one of the best examples of its architectural type in the region, and was acquired by the Historic Buildings Trust shortly before the Second World War. In recent years it has served as the residence of the warden of the nearby Wildlife Study Centre. (Robert Sand)

Above: Willy Lott's cottage at Flatford, Suffolk, immortalized in John Constable's picture, The Haywain. Probably captured for the first time in another colour medium by Robert Sand on a summer day in 1944. The picture was taken from nearby Flatford Mill. (Robert Sand)

Left: Lake Windermere, in the summer of 1945, a panorama from Orrest Head with Scafell Pike, Langdale and Borrowdale Fells in the distance. Below is the hutted camp at Low Wood built for workers employed at the wartime factory at White Cross Bay. This was built by Shorts in 1942, mainly for flying-boat heavy repairs and overhaul, although 35 Sunderlands were built at the works. The top of the hangars can be seen at the water's edge and four Sunderlands, in their all-white Coastal Command finish, can be seen at anchor on the lake. (Robert Astrella)

Left: Another view from Orrest Head looking south-west over Lake Windermere. As with most of his photographs reproduced in this book, Robert Astrella used a Speed Graphic camera. (Robert Astrella)

THE HIGH ROAD

US military installations in Scotland were few but most American servicemen and servicewomen soon discovered that you did not have to go to Scotland to meet Scots. England was well colonized by folk from the northern part of Britain and their social mores were popularly embraced by southerners. Nevertheless, Scotland was a destination high on the list of GIs with a long leave – Edinburgh and Loch Lomond being the main attractions. In fact, most of the Americans seen in these places during the war years were visitors from bases in the south. While those of Scots descent had an understandable desire to see the land of their forefathers, the main draw was the romance with which the Scots have so successfully enveloped and presented their history.

Right: Grey and gaunt against the sky, Edinburgh Castle, viewed from the Lothian Road end of Princes Street Gardens. (Cal Sloan)

It took resolution, patience and endurance to venture to the far north by rail in wartime and all too often those that managed it found, as have many visitors before and since, that low cloud and persistent rain denied them a true appreciation of the unique beauty of the Highlands. Some were fortunate, in particular the intrepid tandem cyclists who found clear skies for a few spring days in 1945. Even their photographs, taken during their journey through remote places, occasionally show the marks of wartime. Few places in the United Kingdom were immune.

Above: The rooftops of Edinburgh. A view from the Outlook Tower with a line of spires; the Tolbooth church and the twelfth-century St Giles' Cathedral with its distinctive crown-like lantern tower. (Cal Sloan)

Left: Another view from the Outlook Tower, east-south-east towards Edinburgh University and Arthur's Seat with the spire of the Tolbooth Church in the left foreground. (Cal Sloan)

Left: The Pets Cemetery for dogs of the garrison at Edinburgh Castle. Looking down towards the junction of Castle and Princes Street and the statue of Thomas Guthrie (1803–83) a local preacher and philanthropist who advocated compulsory education. (Cal Sloan)

Right: The Esplanade, where pre- and post-war the famous Edinburgh Tattoo was held, looking towards the Outlook Tower, in the autumn of 1943. It could be any Sunday afternoon at Edinburgh Castle, but the red cross marked ambulances provide an indication of wartime. (Cal Sloan)

Left: The Floral Clock in Edinburgh's West Princes Street Gardens had a patriotic border in 1944, bedding plants spelling out 'USA', 'Britain', 'China' and 'USSR'. Each year some 20,000 plants are used on the clock's zinc hand and the face to create a theme, usually changed annually. (Cal Sloan)

Left: A sailor admires Mons Meg while two RAF officers admire the view from Edinburgh Castle. Mons Meg was made at Mollance, Galloway and was once seized by the English and held in the Tower of London for more than a century before being restored to Scotland. (Cal Sloan)

Right: Strollers in East Princes Street Gardens soak up the spring sunshine on a Sunday afternoon in 1944. Looking east towards the North Bridge with the City Chambers high on the right and the smoke haze rising over Waverley Station below. (Cal Sloan)

Right: Looking over the roof of Waverley Station towards Calton Hill, with the obelisk erected in 1844 in memory of political martyrs, situated in a burial ground that contains the statue of Abraham Lincoln erected in memory of Scots Americans who died during the War between the States. Behind this is the telescope-like Nelson Memorial built after his victory at Trafalgar where his fleet defeated the combined fleets of France and Spain. (Robert Sand)

Below: A wartime steamer trip on Loch Lomond. The *Prince Edward* with Saturday sightseers leaving Balloch. (Cal Sloan)

Right: *Prince Edward* makes its smoky way north with a good number of GIs among the passengers. The vessel, built in 1911, was operated jointly by the London Midland and Scottish and the London and North-Eastern Railway Companies whose lines met at Balloch. (Cal Sloan)

Right: Empty rest stations at Holyrood House at 4.40 p.m. as clouds roll up to hide the spring sun. This royal residence was built on the site of an abbey by James IV at the end of the fifteenth century. (Cal Sloan)

Left: Loch Lomond, claimed to be the most beautiful inland water in Britain, and one of the largest, being 24 miles long and some five miles at its widest point. The wall, in this view towards Earls Seat, has received white paint as a safety aid in blackout driving. (Cal Sloan)

Right: Blackfaces, renowned for their long straight fleece. An unusually sunny day for the Highlands, with Ben Lomond, 3,192 feet, in the distance. (Cal Sloan)

Below: Inverbeg Hotel, on the western side of Loch Lomond near the head of Glen Douglas, in the spring of 1944. Wartime has its mark here, the painted out Inverbeg on the hotel in the cause of security should the invaders come. (Cal Sloan)

Right: Near the rough stone seat, inscribed as 'Rest And Be Thankful' at the top of the pass from Glen Croe on the road to Cairndow, Argyll. Sergeant Cal Sloan took a rest and a picture of Joe Harris on the tandem they used to explore the Western Highlands. (Cal Sloan)

Right: The sixteenth-century Dundarave Castle overlooking Loch Fyne had been restored as a home. (Cal Sloan)

Left: A splash of bluebells and daffodils in the park at Inveraray Castle, 1945. The seat of the Dukes of Argyll, the neo-gothic castle was completed in 1770 close to the site of an older castle, and houses one of the most interesting collections of art and historic artefacts in Scotland. (Cal Sloan)

Right: Inveraray on Loch Fyne, one of the most attractive small towns in western Scotland, was largely re-built in the eighteenth century by the Duke of Argyll. The GIs stopped on the A86 at a point where many tourists before and since have photographed the town. A front was rolling in from the south-west and threatening rain. (Cal Sloan)

Far right: The snow clings to the summit of Ben Lui (3,708 feet) viewed from the A82 near Tyndrum on an unusually clear and cloud-free day in the summer of 1944. (Cal Sloan)

Right: The Connel Ferry bridge at the Falls of Lora, looking north-east towards 1,145-foot Na Maoilean. Built in 1903, the bridge combined both railway and road, users of the latter paying a toll, which outraged local farmers. Even so, it was preferable to the ferry which could be dangerous in bad weather. The railway and the toll were removed post-war, but were still in place when this photograph was taken in 1944. Beyond, on the Moss of Achnacree are huts occupied by the Royal Air Force; immediately to the left of the bridge on the far side was the only maintained airfield on the west coast of the Highlands. (Cal Sloan)

Left: The higher crests of Britain's highest mountain, the 4,406-foot Ben Nevis, are often hidden by cloud. It is best viewed from the north-west as in this photograph from a train near Corpach, on Loch Eil on a dull day in September 1944. (Robert Sand)

Below: Kilchurn Castle, built in the fifteenth century by the Campbell clan, was abandoned in the eighteenth century and then ruined by gales. Loch Awe stretches away south-west for 23 miles. Sergeants Sloan and Harris were let in to the ruin for half a crown by an old lady who lived in a near-by cottage. They wondered if this was some personal enterprise, but it was considered well worth the half dollar. (Cal Sloan)

Right: Stacks of fodder thatched and netted down for the winter on a croft near Dalmally, in the spring of 1945. (Cal Sloan)

Left: The approach to Killin village at the western end of Loch Tay, seat of the clan Mac-Nab in medieval times. The River Dochart bubbles along and in the distance 3,984-foot Ben Lawers dominates the skyline. The War Memorial beside the A827 carries 28 names of those of the district who fell in the First World War. Since this photograph was taken the names of six local men killed in the Second World War have been added. (Cal Sloan)

Above left: Highland cattle near Stirling. The photographer was told that the breed was the ancestor of the Texas Longhorn. (Cal Sloan)

Above right: Inverness Cathedral and Courts, looking southwest across the River Ness from the Castle. This pleasant vista belies the fact that much industry flourished in this city, including a plant that carried out welding fabrications for the Pluto pipeline. (Robert Sand)

Right: The comparatively modern red stone Inverness Castle, a Victorian construction (1834) built on the site of a much earlier fortress that guarded the river crossing. Put to municipal use, it housed the police and the County Courts of Justice in 1944. Photographed from the west side of the Ness with the road bridge in the foreground. (Robert Sand)

Left: Cottages in Glen Lyon thatched with reed which was not so common in Scotland as in England. (Cal Sloan)

Right: Looking down Loch Ailort from the Mallaig-Fort William railway with the cloud-capped Rois-Bheinn in the distance, September 1944. The locomotive driver bought beer for the cameraman and his fellow at one of the station stops. (Robert Sand)

Lower right: The Porteous farm near Portree, Skye on a windswept September day in 1944. A small plot of oats is being harvested beyond the rough moor. A boy of about 15, James Porteous, took visiting GIs Herb Heichelbech and Robert Sand round the farm; 'His speech was like music.' (Robert Sand)

Left: The beauty of the Highlands. An ancient bridge spanning a rushing mountain burn among the fresh leaved birch trees. (Cal Sloan)

CITIES AND TOWNS

The cities and towns that came under the camera lens of American service personnel were predominantly those in close proximity to their military bases, places reached in an hour or two. Thus the colour photographs that follow are mostly from the south, south-west and south-east of England with, understandably, the heaviest concentration being in East Anglia where the US Army Air Force's bases endured longest. Photographers were drawn chiefly to antiquities, cathedrals, churches and castles, the likes of which were not to be seen in their own land. Anything that pre-dated the foundation of the United States was of great interest. And, of course, public houses – pubs – must be the front runner of all subjects, for both colour and monochrome snaps. After the wide roads and spaciousness of most US towns, those in Britain seem decidedly cramped and crowded, to say nothing of being shabby and grimy from wartime neglect.

Right: Norwich was in the midst of the American invasion and its fine cathedral received much attention from the visitors. This view from the castle was taken in the winter of 1944–45. (Albert Krassman)

Left: The spire of Norwich Cathedral, 1944. The city was heavily bombed during the so-called Baedeker raids of 1942. Some windows had been blown out by bombs on 2 December 1940, but on 27 June 1942 an incendiary bomb from a sneak raider struck the North Transept roof and caused severe fire damage although the blaze was soon extinguished. (Albert Krassman)

Above: Edith Cavell's simple grave beside the curving wall of St Luke's Chapel, Norwich Cathedral, as it appeared in 1945. On 12 October 1915 Edith Cavell, a nurse at a Brussels hospital, was shot by a German firing squad for having helped and sheltered British soldiers. Her remains were re-interred beside the South Transept of Norwich Cathedral in 1919, Edith Cavell having been a native of Norfolk. (Albert Krassman)

Left: The box-like Norman castle at Norwich, overlooking the large cattle market, seen beneath fading aircraft contrails in a clear winter sky. The castle served as a city and county museum. (Albert Krassman)

Below: The palatial Norwich City Hall, opened in 1939, with the Roman Catholic church on the skyline. The City Hall received only moderate blast and splinter damage in the mini-Blitz of April 1942. During the war Luftwaffe bombing of Norwich destroyed 2,082 buildings and caused damage to 28,272 other properties, of which 2,651 were severely damaged. (Albert Krassman)

Above: The Cow Tower, an ancient defensive position at Norwich on the bend of the Wensum. Built in 1390 it is believed to be the earliest artillery fortification in Britain. (Albert Krassman)

Above right: Coal scuffles and metal *objets d'art* attract passers by, including a US officer, at a stall in Norwich's Market Square. The market, one of the oldest in England, dates from the twelfth century. (George Parker)

Right: The Octagon of imposing Ely Cathedral was built *circa* 1340 following the collapse of the original Norman tower. The eight massive wood pillars, 63 feet long with girths 2 feet 7 inches by 3 feet 4 inches, support some four hundred tons of glass and lead. A monk, Alan de Walsingham, was the architect for this extraordinary feat of engineering. (Cal Sloan)

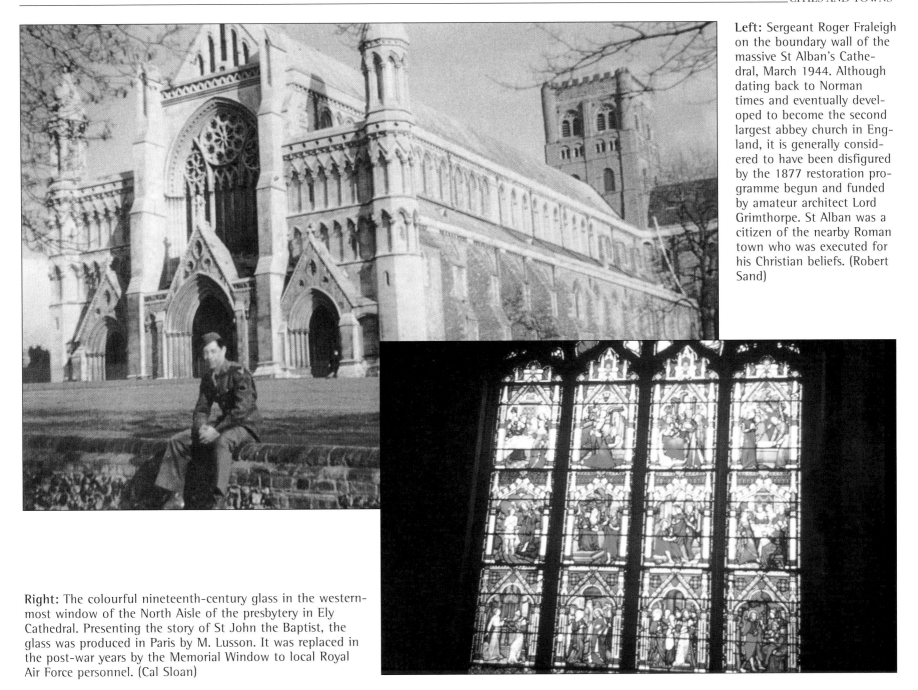

Left: Sergeant Roger Fraleigh on the boundary wall of the massive St Alban's Cathedral, March 1944. Although dating back to Norman times and eventually developed to become the second largest abbey church in England, it is generally considered to have been disfigured by the 1877 restoration programme begun and funded by amateur architect Lord Grimthorpe. St Alban was a citizen of the nearby Roman town who was executed for his Christian beliefs. (Robert Sand)

Right: The colourful nineteenth-century glass in the westernmost window of the North Aisle of the presbytery in Ely Cathedral. Presenting the story of St John the Baptist, the glass was produced in Paris by M. Lusson. It was replaced in the post-war years by the Memorial Window to local Royal Air Force personnel. (Cal Sloan)

Left: 'The Fighting Cocks', St Albans. A pose against the oldest inhabited licensed inn in England made a worthy souvenir photograph to take home to the folk in the USA. Dating from the beginning of the seventeenth century, the little round house is said to have been part of a monastic building that stood on the site. At one time it was used as an arena for fighting cocks until this was finally banned. (Robert Sand)

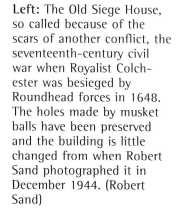

Bottom left: Colchester Castle. The Norman Keep built on the site of the Roman Temple sacked in AD 61 by Queen Boadicea and the Iceni tribe. Photographed on 30 August 1944; the 'S' for Shelter sign and the RAF uniform underline the date. (Robert Sand)

Left: The Old Siege House, so called because of the scars of another conflict, the seventeenth-century civil war when Royalist Colchester was besieged by Roundhead forces in 1648. The holes made by musket balls have been preserved and the building is little changed from when Robert Sand photographed it in December 1944. (Robert Sand)

Above: Pub crawl, the off-duty serviceman's favourite occupation. A half of bitter from the Tap Room at the back of 'The Cups Hotel', High Street, Colchester in August 1944. The hotel was demolished in the Sixties. (Robert Sand)

Above right: 'The Rose and Crown Inn', East Gates, Colchester, restored to its original Tudor style just before the Second World War by a philanthropic enthusiast, Grace Faithful Roper. The photographer and his friend entered and waited in vain to be served, then realized that it was no longer in use as a public house. (Robert Sand)

Right: A GI and an RAF acquaintance head for the 'Nelson Head' pub in the Dutch Quarter of Colchester, Britain's oldest recorded town. Fifty years on the pub and most of the commercial establishments have gone from West Stockwell Street, and the buildings are now largely residential. (Robert Sand)

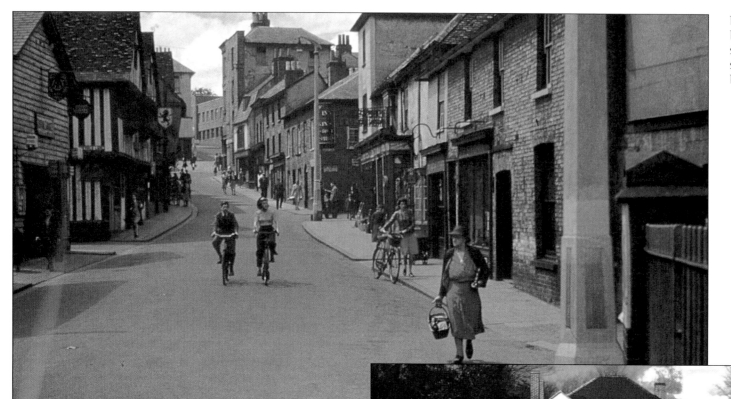

Right: Lieutenant J. S. Hollinger, a Marauder bomber pilot, stops to eat his fish and chips, the original takeaway and one of the few unrationed food items – but it was first come, first served for stocks were limited. The bungalow is the head gardener's of Castle Gardens, adjacent to the park in Bishop's Stortford. (Jack Havener)

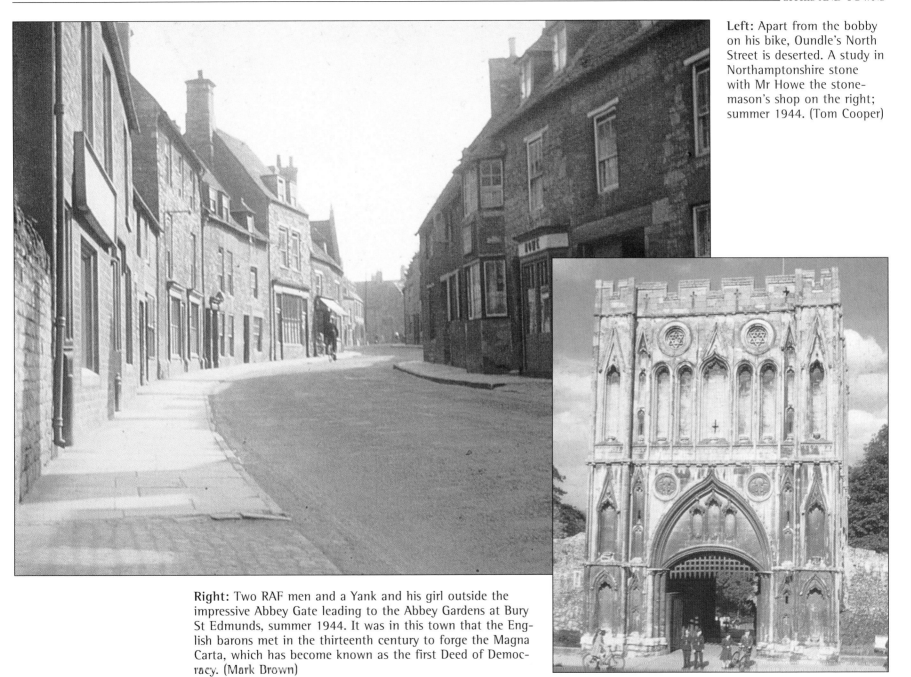

Right: Two RAF men and a Yank and his girl outside the impressive Abbey Gate leading to the Abbey Gardens at Bury St Edmunds, summer 1944. It was in this town that the English barons met in the thirteenth century to forge the Magna Carta, which has become known as the first Deed of Democracy. (Mark Brown)

Left: Henley-on-Thames's main street with the sixteenth-century tower of the church of St Paul in the summer of 1945. The town is well known as the venue of the Henley Royal Regatta held each July. (Robert Astrella)

Right: The A423 bridge at Henley-on-Thames looking towards The Angel Hotel, which offered free mooring along its waterfront to encourage patrons. (Robert Astrella)

Left: The Thames at St Helen's Wharf, Abingdon and another inn. The Abbey towers above the tall chimney stacks. The number and complexity of British chimneys intrigued GIs who had seen nothing like them in the States. (Robert Astrella)

Right: A between-the-wars council estate of purely functional architecture in red brick, tile and stone dash. Pupils from a primary school out walking rest beside the river path at Saxon Road, Abingdon. Possibly these youngsters are now grandmothers and grandfathers. (Robert Astrella)

Left: The elaborate West Window of Worcester Cathedral which was inserted during restoration in Victorian times. The infamous King John was laid to rest here in 1216. Worcester was an infantry training centre for the British Army during the Second World War. (Robert Astrella)

Right: Not quite the British equivalent to the Drum Majorettes of an American ball game, but these 'gals with bagpipes' drew plenty of GI interest. During wartime, martial entertainment was considered good for public morale and a show of this nature was regularly arranged for most fair-sized towns. This ATS pipe band is seen performing on Parker's Piece at Cambridge. The Auxiliary Territorial Service, which had a strength of 212,000 in 1944 when this photograph was taken, was the largest of the British women's services. (Cal Sloan)

Right: The Queen drives by. This photograph is believed to have been taken on 12 July 1945 when Her Majesty, having an engagement at the Civil Resettlement Planning Headquarters at Hatfield, was passing through Hitchin. (Cal Sloan)

Below: In 1944 the main street of Lavenham in Suffolk was far from the picture postcard scene for which this little town would be famous in the late twentieth century. By the fifth year of war the plaster fronts of Elizabethan houses were stained and cracked. The threat of invasion had receded, but the concrete anti-tank blocks still reposed on the pavements. This house stands near the junction with Bears Lane. (Mark Brown)

Above: Flags out for VE-Day, 8 May 1945, in the little market town of Eye, Suffolk. The memorial in the centre of the town was for the dead of the 1914-18 War. (Arnold Delmonico)

Left: Diversification was the theme at Deacons the builders on the east side of the southern end of Lavenham High Street. Repairing tumbrils or burying the town's dead was all in the day's work. A Jeep waits for the photographer. (Mark Brown)

Right: A Liberty Truck full of US servicemen from a nearby airbase drives up the main street of Bungay, Suffolk, having passed through the Butter Cross on a summer evening in 1944. (George Parker)

Left: Saint Peter and Saint Paul, Lavenham, a particularly fine church for such a small community, resulting from the wealth of the wool weaving industry that flourished during the seventeenth century. (M Brown)

Above: The wandering GI was bound to stop before such a tombstone as this at Manningtree, Essex and wonder if the deceased were any relation to the famous American namesake. (Robert Sand)

Right: Nardi's Fish and Chips brightens this otherwise drab street in Aberdeen. The 'S' sign indicates the nearest air raid shelter. (George Parker)

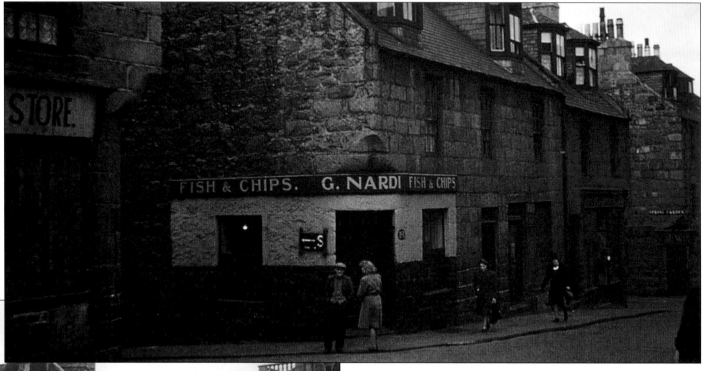

Left: Cobblestones and grey houses on the outskirts of Aberdeen. Only the white paint on the kerbstones makes this a wartime scene. (George Parker)

THE RURAL PANORAMA

Before the 1939-45 conflict British villages well removed from urban conurbations enjoyed a degree of isolation and a pace of life little changed from a century before, passing motor vehicles being few and far between. With the war and Britain's isolation, remote places in the countryside suddenly had to play host to a variety of military installations, particularly in the south and east of the island. Mansions and estates were requisitioned and many farms disappeared under acres of concrete as hundreds of airfields were constructed. The majority of US military bases were in rural England where the newcomers often outnumbered the natives by as much as twenty to one.

To those from a comparatively young nation, where the general trend was for advancement in all spheres of life, the English country scene appeared

Right: The spire of Kimbolton church protrudes among the greenery of the Huntingdonshire countryside. A view from one of the domestic sites serving the airfield to the north as a farmer and his wife take an evening stroll in June 1944. (Edmund Lutz)

decidedly backward or at least 'quaint'. A distinct pastoral beauty was acknowledged by many, but the photography was again directed chiefly at ancient buildings. Thatched houses were a particular attraction, also churches and, of course, pubs. It is not that the average GI was a drinking man, many could not bear to touch the 'flat warm' English beers. Rather the interest in obtaining a pictorial record was because the pub, representing the main centre of social contact in small villages, had no true equivalent in the United States. Those with Kodachrome in their cameras undoubtedly took the first ever colour photographs of these country subjects.

Left: Rural England from the air; the distinctive lush greenness of the small hedge-lined fields, with grain crops turning to gold in this June 1944 photograph taken from a Liberator bomber. (George Parker)

Right: The view from the Abbey tower at Dorchester-on-Thames, north-west over the rooftops of the village towards the Thames. A popular hostelry, The George Hotel, is prominent in the main street, and the Victorian lych gate leading to the Abbey is in the foreground. (Robert Astrella)

Below: Sinodun Hills, popularly known as the Wittenham Clumps, rise 400 and 373 feet from the Thames valley, the southernmost being the site of an Iron Age fort. Viewed here south-west from Dorchester Abbey across the village allotments and C. V. Bowditch's dairy farm meadows. (Robert Astrella)

Right: Thirteenth-century stained glass in Dorchester Abbey. The great East Window with heraldic shields and figures relate to St Birinus who founded the original cathedral in 635. The current building, on the same site, dates from the twelfth century. In medieval times it was the major cathedral in the upper Thames valley. (Robert Astrella)

Right: The Old Grammar School at Thame, Oxfordshire became almshouses. The zig-zag of electric wires common in most small communities in 1944, would eventually be put underground. (Robert Astrella)

Right: A GI makes his way back to base from 'The Crown' at Litlington, Cambridgeshire. Britain's red 'phone booths' and their 'A' and 'B' button operation intrigued and frustrated American servicemen, as did the operator's 'you're through' before they had had the call. (Cal Sloan)

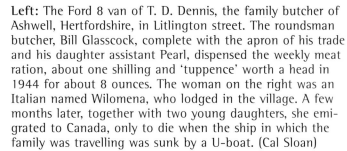

Left: The Ford 8 van of T. D. Dennis, the family butcher of Ashwell, Hertfordshire, in Litlington street. The roundsman butcher, Bill Glasscock, complete with the apron of his trade and his daughter assistant Pearl, dispensed the weekly meat ration, about one shilling and 'tuppence' worth a head in 1944 for about 8 ounces. The woman on the right was an Italian named Wilomena, who lodged in the village. A few months later, together with two young daughters, she emigrated to Canada, only to die when the ship in which the family was travelling was sunk by a U-boat. (Cal Sloan)

Right: An English country garden with wisteria in full bloom; 7 May 1945. Stourbank at Nayland, Suffolk, an old coaching inn turned private house, often entertained US service personnel. The girl is Janet Huston, an American Red Cross operative from a local airfield. (Robert Sand)

Right: Most sizeable English villages had a resident general practitioner and this is the doctor's house in Nayland village, Suffolk, May 1945. The female driver of the carrier's vehicle is being 'chatted up' by two soldiers. (Robert Sand)

Below right: On the Essex side of the River Stour, the sixteenth-century building that once served as the toll booth for travellers on the main London to Norwich highway who wanted to cross the bridge, was restored in the nineteen-thirties by Grace Faithful Roper and used as a guest house. Postwar it was acquired by Gerald Milsom and Le Talbooth, Dedham, has become one of the best-known restaurants in the country. Robert Sand took this photograph on 27 May 1945. He recorded the occasion as follows: ' We were looking for a place to stay the night, and this looked perfect. A most special inducement was a most lovely, winsome girl (standing almost invisible in the shadowed doorway) who told us the inn was full. One of the very rare times an English girl looked at us without that look of sheer boredom, "My God, another Yank." We were saddened to leave. If I ever get to England again, must look this place up. Will tell her she is remembered. (Robert Sand)

Top left: Tile and plaster; typical agricultural workers' cottages near Woodbridge, Suffolk. Woollen blankets are on the washing line to make the most of a drying day. (Mark Brown)

Above: At Christmas 1944 a period of extreme winter weather set in. The trees and hedges were hung with hoar-frost from the freezing fog. A Jeep comes along a road widened for use by the traffic of Wormingford airfield, the domestic sites in the vicinity accounting for the jumble of overhead cables. (Robert Sand)

Left: Grain stacks on a Wormingford farm behind the barrack site in the freezing conditions of Boxing Day 1944. (Robert Sand)

THATCH

Right: Thatch in south-west England. A pink chestnut in full bloom beside the gate-house in the picture postcard village of Cockington, a mere mile from the seaside resort of Torquay in Devon which, in wartime, was a services convalescent area. Photographed on 25 April 1945. (Robert Sand)

Left: Thatched roofs were a curiosity for many Americans. This cottage at Homersfield, Suffolk on the road between Mendham and St Cross, was near a village defensive strongpoint. The tank obstacles in the garden on the left were still there 50 years later. (George Parker)

Far left: A thatcher at his trade on a cottage at Nuthampstead, Hertford-shire, in March 1944. The concrete slab path was a wartime addition along this village road to allow men at the surrounding airbase to walk unmuddied to their mess hall. (Robert Sand)

Left: A true worker's cottage of worn thatch and crumb-ling plaster near Bungay, Suffolk, in the summer of 1944. No piped water or electricity, and cooking required a solid fuel fire all the year round – as the smoking chimneys show. (Mark Brown)

Left: The recently thatched cottage of Mrs Kate Barrell in Park Lane, Langham, Essex. Her son, Leonard, can be seen in the well-kept gar-den on this August 1944 day. Only the coiled barbed wire along the hedgeline mars this rural scene, for just a few yards to the right was an airfield perimeter track and the photographer was standing on the airfield to take this shot. (Mark Brown)

Right: Rustic charm. A vine-decked cottage on the low road at Clifton Hampden, Oxfordshire, summer 1944. (Robert Astrella)

Left: A beautifully kept cottage garden in south-east Oxfordshire, but the roof was in a sorry state. Note the tradesman's 'bike', such bicycles were much sought after as personal transport during the war years; the sturdy front carrier took a useful load. (Robert Astrella)

Right: Spick and span. No labourer's cottage this at Drayton St Leonard, Oxford-shire. An upgraded resi-dence, it was occupied by an RAF Wing Commander serv-ing at a local airfield when the photograph was taken in the spring of 1944. (Robert Astrella)

Left: Twin thatched gate lodges in Little Milton, Oxfordshire on the B4013 road. For the nearest, accessories include letter box, bird table and dog kennel. These dwellings had changed little 50 years after they were photographed in April 1944. (Robert Astrella)

RIVER SCENE

Below: A pleasure boat trip on the river was a popular way of spending a wartime Sunday afternoon. This is *Majestic* steaming its way up the Thames near Wallingford. (Robert Astrella)

Right: With strict food rationing, river fishing was not just fun, although in this case with a stick, a piece of string and a bent pin, a catch can have been little more than a schoolboy's dream. The River Cam, in the summer of 1944. (Cal Sloan)

Bottom right: A more professional attempt to fill out the larder under the shade of a willow on the Cam. A warm summer day near Cambridge in 1944. (Cal Sloan)

Left: Flags out for VE-Day at Riverside, Burcot, Oxford-shire, which served as a convalescent home for soldiers when this photograph was taken in 1945. (Robert Astrella)

Left: Bird Place, Cleeve on the Thames was struck by a bomb earlier in the war and an occupant was killed. When photographed in May 1945 it had been rebuilt and no visible scars remained. (Robert Astrella)

Above: Thames Bank, Goring, Oxfordshire; a rest home for Belgian servicemen and, on the day on which the photograph was taken, warm enough for some hardy fellow to take to the water. (Robert Astrella)

Right: The first day of sailing at Wivenhoe on the River Colne, Essex since wartime restrictions were lifted; 19 May 1945. (Robert Sand)

Above: Yanks were good with kids and, as this photograph proves, their presence did not take long to gather a small crowd. These youngsters found Sergeant Phil Moose painting a watercolour of the boats at Wivenhoe. (Robert Sand)

FARMING

Top right: Commercial flower growing was banned during hostilities, but in the summer of 1945 this plot at Feering, Essex, bloomed once more with yellow calendula, pink godetia and white alyssum. The plot, owned by Sid Taylor, a railway man, was worked in his spare time with his family. Photographed from a London-bound train, the parish church is prominent in the background; from the top of its tower three wartime airfields were visible. (Robert Sand)

Right: Shades of pre-war agricultural depression. Dilapidated barns at Jenkins Farm, Wormingford, Essex; 14 April 1944. The house faced the airfield built in the parish. (Robert Sand)

Right: A spade lug, iron-wheeled Standard Fordson tractor, which ran on Tractor Vaporising Oil (paraffin), was the wartime workhorse on most farms. This one has a Land Army girl driver, her task rib-rolling winter wheat to consolidate the soil, break clods and induce tillering. She has a roadside spectator. Oxfordshire, 1944. (Robert Astrella)

Left: Typical ramshackle small farm buildings of the period and strawed stackyard, near Lavenham, Suffolk. The sheep's parsley was in bloom on this May day in 1944. (Mark Brown)

Right: The scythe was still to be found on most farms. These men are swinging theirs against a scarlet growth of poppies on land near Eye airfield. Liberator bombers parked on their hardstands can be seen in the background. (Mark Brown)

Left: A wheat field at Well-house Farm, Wormingford overlooking the Stour valley, decked out with poppies – spring 1944. (Robert Sand)

Right: Cows among the buttercups. Red Polls on a Hertfordshire farm, spring 1944. This popular breed would gradually become rare during the later years of the twentieth century. The sun was warm enough on the day this photograph was taken for the major tormentor of bovines, flies, to be present in strength. (Cal Sloan)

Right: The Duke of Gloucester's prize Guernsey bull at Barnwell, Northants, summer 1944. A Land Army girl in standard uniform looks on. (Tom Cooper)

Below, near right: A field of shocked wheat sheaves at Wormingford on 4 August 1944. The previous day, when a few farm men entered the field and started standing the sheaves, they were suddenly joined by a throng of American mechanics and the job was finished in record time. The photograph was taken from outside the propeller shop on the adjoining airfield, whence the frustrated farmers had volunteered their services. The sails of a ruined windmill can be seen beyond the farmhouse. (Robert Sand)

Far right: Large acreage farms were fortunate to obtain some of the more modern rubber-tyred tractors imported from the United States. This International Farmall Model A hauls a distributor for dispensing nitrogenous fertilizer on a crop of wheat at Mount Farm, Drayton St Leonard, Oxfordshire; spring 1943. (Robert Astrella)

Below: Wheat sheaves being unloaded on to an elevator or pitcher at a stack beside Mount Farm airfield. The tractor is an imported International W6. (Robert Astrella)

Right: Beautifully shaped round stacks of wheat at Mount Farm. A skilled job, and the stacker took a pride in his work, for any deviation would bring caustic comment from his workmates. (Robert Astrella)

Right: Pitching oat sheaves at College Farm, Litlington, August 1944. Jim Carter holds *Short*, a noble Percheron, by the bridle. Schoolboys could earn sixpence a day leading a horse at harvest time. Cecil Pell stacks the cart while Albert Lawrence pitches. (Cal Sloan)

Left: In the fields beyond the oat stubble the Nissen huts serving as a communal mess hall for Steeple Morden airfield, stand alien to this rural scene. Ken Stoten on the tumbril and Albert Lawrence pitching the sheaves. *Prince* moved forward on command of mouth. (Cal Sloan)

Right: Albert Lawrence, Ken Stoten and Cecil Pell on the stack while Fred Ingney, the farmer, forks the sheaves from the cart. Building a stack at College Farm, Litlington, St Catherine's church tower in the background. (Cal Sloan)

Right: An idyllic pose. John and Joy Gilson, children of a farm worker bottle feeding an orphan lamb on Charles Northern's farm at Rockingham, Northamptonshire in the summer of 1944. (Milton Holley)

Far right: *Punch* out to grass at Bury Farm, Litlington. There were few British arable farms that did not have carthorses during the war years, the antithesis of the situation half a century on when a heavy horse is a rare sight. (Cal Sloan)

Left: Suffolk Punches, the most popular breed of cart-horse in East Anglia, in a meadow at Wormingford Hall, Essex; *Juno* and *Mayo*, born a month apart; June 1945. (Robert Sand)

Below: The farmer got a helping hand from GIs at the adjacent air base to thresh this wheat stack at Abbey Farm, Flixton, Suffolk. A steam engine operated by contractors provided the motive power for most threshing combinations. A dirty, dusty, noisy and uncomfortable task. (George Parker)

Right: Threshing wheat at Wormingford on 9 April 1945. Farmers had to wait their turn for the threshing machinery, and often had to book its services months in advance. (Robert Sand)

MANSIONS

Right: Suffolk Punches graze beside the lake in Redgrave Hall Park, spring 1944. The Hall and grounds served as a US General Hospital during hostilities. On the south side of the lake a prisoner-of-war camp was established. (Arnold Delmonico)

Left: Playford Hall, near Woodbridge, Suffolk. A moated Elizabethan mansion with eighteenth-century alterations was owned by the Marquis of Bristol and served as the billet for personnel from nearby Martlesham Heath airfield. When photographed in January 1945, it housed the officers of the 360th Fighter Squadron. Thomas Clarkson, prominent in obtaining the abolition of slavery, died at the hall in 1846, aged 85. It is believed the house stands on the site of the home of an eminent fifteenth-century knight, Sir George Felbrigg. (Herb Rutland)

Left: Summer blossom in the lily pond of the neglected formal garden at Lord Iveagh's Elveden Hall, Suffolk in 1944. Used as the headquarters site for the USAAF's 3rd Bombardment Division, prefabricated huts were erected in the grounds and lines were strung out across the gardens to dry laundry. (Mark Brown)

Right: Halton Hall, a small dilapidated mansion adjacent to Halesworth airfield in Suffolk. In the autumn of 1944, when photographed, it was in use by the USAAF staff. The building was demolished post-war. (Robert Buck)

Below right: The building of Easton Lodge, begun in 1590 by the first Lord Maynard, was owned by the family until the last Viscount Maynard died in 1865. The property then passed to his eldest grand-daughter, then aged three, who eventually married and became Countess of Warwick. This formidable lady entertained lavishly and among her frequent guests at Easton Lodge was the Prince of Wales, later King Edward VII. However, the Countess became an ardent socialist, supporting many progressive causes; but it was the austerity of a Socialist government post-war that caused her descendants to have the building demolished in 1948, ten years after her death. When this photograph was taken in May 1944, the occupants were officers of the US bomber organization occupying the airfield built in the adjoining deer park. (John Meyers)

Above: Magnificent Flixton Hall, near Bungay, home of the Adair family. Post-war, the upkeep could no longer be met and, like many similar mansions, it was demolished. Photographed here across parkland butter-cups from the nearby airfield complex of Bungay. (Albert Krassman)

CHURCHES

Left: Many US servicemen were fascinated by the old and substantially built churches that were to be found in almost every English village. This particularly fine example is at Woolpit, Suffolk. (Mark Brown)

Right: The fine porch of St Mary's, Woolpit. (Mark Brown)

Left: St Mary's, Rickinghall Inferior, Suffolk. A scene from the south-west corner. The barbed wire was laid in 1940 to impede the invader when the village was a defensive strongpoint. (Mark Brown)

Right: St Peter's Church at St Peter South Elmham, near Halesworth, Suffolk. (Albert Krassman)

Far right: The airmen at nearby Snetterton Heath airfield paid for this restored chapel and stained glass window in memory of their dead. Dedicated by the Bishop of Norwich in November 1944, the window in Quidenham Church depicts an airman and insignia of the 96th Bomb Group and its squadrons, the first such memorial in an English church. (Eugene Blue)

Above: The round tower church of St Andrews, Quidenham, winter 1944. (Eugene Blue)

Right: Rattlesden church, spring 1945. The American bomber base on the edge of this Suffolk village brought a number of marriages of its personnel to local girls. One US airman who married in the church in 1945 settled in the village post-war. There were no wedding bells at these wartime marriages as the ringing of church bells was banned from June 1940 except as a warning of invasion. The one exception was 15 November 1942 when special dispensation was given for church bells to ring for the victory at El Alamein. (Mark Brown)

Right: A church near Polebrook, Northants in an idyllic setting. (Tom Cooper)

PUBS

Left: A Thames-side pub at Goring, 'The Old Leathern Bottel', on a warm June day in 1945. The water from a natural spring on the west side of this building was said to have medicinal properties, but the innkeepers preferred to sell you beer. The Great Western Railway from London to Bristol ran on the embankment behind the pub. (Robert Astrella)

127

Left: Shillingford Bridge Hotel on the A329 from Wallingford to Dorchester-on-Thames. The yellow disc bearing the numeral '70' is a Royal Engineers warning that the bridge had a maximum weight limit of 70 tons for vehicles. Reckoned to be one of the finest Thames bridges, it was built in 1827 and partly rebuilt in 1906. Discarded anti-tank obstacles stand nearby; spring 1945. (Robert Astrella)

Right: The Castle Hotel, Benson, an eighteenth-century inn and favourite hostelry of men from the RAF airfield nearby. The car has masked headlights to comply with the blackout regulations. (Robert Astrella)

Left: Just down the road from The George, a fifteenth-century inn in Dorchester on Thames, British soldiers wait beside The White Hart sign for transport back to camp. (Robert Astrella)

Right: Pub names intrigued American servicemen. The 'Half Butt Inn' at Great Horkesley, Essex, just up the road from the brewers who owned it, was a popular haunt for GIs. They were moved by the dedication of the middle-aged landlady who kept the pub open as normal despite her husband having died earlier in the day, his body still being on the premises. (Robert Sand)

Left: 'The Dog' at Easton. A plain building on the A47 highway east of Norwich as it appeared in 1944. Wooden porches with doors were built round the original entrances as a blackout measure. The door into the darkened porch was opened and closed before opening the main door into the lighted pub. Bullards, the brewers, have long since disappeared into history. (George Parker)

Right: 'The Black Swan', Homersfield, Suffolk; a favourite drinking place for American airmen from the nearby airfield at Bungay. (George Parker)

WINDMILLS

Right: Wind or water drove the many country mills that ground the local grain. Newbridge Mill, West Bergholt, Essex was originally a watermill that was converted to steam power, although this motive power did not prevail for long. It was still a working mill on the warm July day in 1945 when this photograph was taken. A few years later it caught fire and was destroyed. (Robert Sand)

Left: Rendered obsolete by later milling technology, an abandoned windmill at Great Haseley beside the B4013 south-west of Thame, Oxfordshire. A building of much interest to US service-men as evidenced by the two leaning against its wall. (Robert Astrella)

Right: Tiptree windmill, Essex, dating from 1775, had steam power back-up added towards the end of the nineteenth century, although sail power contin-ued in intermittent use until 1921. Photographed in May 1945, it had stood silent for many years. Following the Second World War it was converted to a house. (Robert Sand)

Below right: A dilapidated windmill at Birch Green, Essex. Built in the eighteenth century, it was little used in the next century and when this picture was taken in 1944 was in a sorry state of neglect. It was dismantled in 1962. Robert Sand recorded in his diary that the elderly couple in the photograph were sur-prised to see uniformed men: 'Oh are you Americans? There were two other Ameri-cans taking pictures of the windmill.' It transpired that the visit of the 'other Ameri-cans' was during the First World War! (Robert Sand)

Above: Dark-boarded windmill at Madingley Hill in the parish of Coton. Approximately 200 yards west of the site where the American Military Cemetery was created for US military dead of the Second World War, mostly airmen. (Cal Sloan)

COAST AND SEA

Being an island, the sea has always played a prominent part in Britain's history and remains of particular fascination to the nation. In the pre-Second World War days the major holiday destination of the population was the seaside, be it for a day out or a longer stay for the more fortunate. The era of the cheap package holiday and everyman's travel to foreign climes was yet to arrive. In consequence, the American servicemen were often rec-ommended by British acquaintances to visit some coastal resort for fun and relaxation. Those who followed this advice were usually somewhat disillusioned, for the places were dulled by wartime closures and restrictions, while the weather was rarely conducive to exposed contact with sand and sea-especially for those used to the sun-drenched beaches of California or Florida.

Left: The Parade at Penzance in 1943. A view towards the town in sharp contrast to its usual crowded peacetime state. Penzance has the dubious distinction of being the only English town invaded and burned by the Spaniards – in 1595. (Robert Astrella)

Right: Looking more like the Riviera than England, Torquay's palms on a spring day in April 1945, in a view across Tor Bay. (Robert Sand)

Below: An afternoon in the picturesque fishing port of St Ives, Cornwall in 1943. The barrage balloon flies above a naval minesweeper to deter any attack by low-flying aircraft that might chance a hit-and-run raid, a coastal nuisance in 1942-43. (Robert Astrella)

Left: The ancient chapel of St Nicholas on the coast of St Ives was partially destroyed in 1904, apparently by uncautious action of the War Office. The building was restored in 1911 by a local benefactor. (Robert Astrella)

Right: Low tide and no time is lost in gathering seaweed for fertilizer at Marazion, a fishing village three miles east of Penzance. Seaweed, according to species, was also a source of food and iodine. (Robert Astrella)

Right: Sennen Cove, in Cornwall, with its lifeboat station and the most westerly church in England on the hill above. The prefabricated buildings near the shore were used by RAF personnel who manned radar stations in the district. (Robert Astrella)

Left: St Michael's Mount, autumn 1943. The original site of a Benedictine chapel, the castle dates from the fourteenth century. It was privately owned when this photograph was taken, although part commandeered by the military – a gun emplacement can be seen on the seaward tip of the island. In 1954 St Michael's Mount was given to the nation by Lord St Levan, whose forebears had owned the property for 300 years. (Robert Astrella)

Right: Rugged Land's End and its lookout tower was much as it had been in pre-war days when photographed in colour in the autumn of 1943. Only the new block-built generator hut had recently been added to the scene. (Robert Astrella)

Left: Lieutenant Jack Havener peers over the 350-foot high Shakespeare Cliff from which, on clear days, enemy-held France was clearly visible. Behind Havener is the railway from Folkestone to Dover which tunnels through the cliff and became a target for Stukas in 1940. Dover Harbour is filled with landing-craft and three close-hauled balloons can be seen as part of the Dover barrage. The four masts in the distance beyond Dover Castle are those of the Home Chain radar station. (Jack Havener)

Below left: Looking up Castle Street, Dover on a spring day in 1945. The castle was used as a military barracks during the war. (Cal Sloan)

Right: A soldier among the beachcombers might be the only clue to this photograph having been taken in wartime. However, the deserted buildings behind the shoreline were wrecked in Commando training. This is St Margaret's at Cliffe, a few miles north-east of Dover. A house at the far end was owned pre-war by Noel Coward and, later, Ian Fleming. (Cal Sloan)

Far left: It was warm enough on 30 March 1945 for sand castles on Dovercourt's beach. The youngsters were probably unaware of the photographer, who escaped without the usual plea for gum. (Robert Sand)

Left: Dovercourt, Essex, looking north towards Harwich and Felixstowe with its seaplane hangars on the horizon. The remnants of invasion defences in the foreground include a defunct pillbox and the scaffold-like structure at a beach access point, erected to prevent assault boats from closing in at high tide. (Robert Sand)

Below left: A summer evening in Oban, Argyll. McCaig's Folly is prominent above the town and resembles the Coliseum of Rome. Commenced in 1897 by John Stewart McCaig, a banker, who conceived it as a means of providing work for the poor, he spent £5,000 on the construction but the building was never completed. Out of view on the right of this picture is the large RAF flying-boat installation in the Sound of Kerrera. (Cal Sloan)

Left: Under a typical grey sky, shipping in the lower reaches of the Mersey. A photograph taken from the USS *Lincoln Steffins*, a Liberty Ship carrying several hundred US servicemen back to the USA in the summer of 1945. (Robert Sand)

Right: Swans on the Stour estuary at Mistley, Essex, 17 May 1945. The birds still congregate there half a century on, with numbers much increased. The estuary to the right on the Suffolk side was used as a bombing range throughout the war. (Robert Sand)

TRANSPORTATION

Left: A game of skipping. Teenagers in a Harwich street, 30 March 1945. The doorsteps of the terraced houses have been white-washed as an aid to pedestrians in the blackout. Harwich, being an important naval base, maintained street blackouts until the end of the war in Europe. (Robert Sand)

Right: A first look at Britain's railway system. US airmen, newly arrived in Liverpool, wait for a train to take them to southern England. (Stan Wyglendowski)

Modern motive power for road, rail and sea may have originated in Europe, but the wholehearted development in the United States to meet its own transportation requirements took quite a different direction. The sheer magnitude of North America brought a demand for large transports to convey as much as possible over great distances. There spacious towns and cities did not necessitate the restrictions on vehicle size as in Europe. Automotive passenger and goods vehicles, locomotives, rolling stock and commercial river vessels were usually much larger in the United States. In consequence, the GI found the equivalents in Britain small, cramped and often a curiosity. The markedly different vehicles and vessels often drew a camera.

Right: LNER locomotive No. 4411 steams into Royston station on route to London. British locomotives seemed 'dinky' compared with the giants in North America. (Cal Sloan)

Left: A work-worn LMS locomotive pulls through a London suburban station. The extensive British railway system then covered most parts of the island and although public passenger services were maintained throughout the war, travel was at times agonizingly slow. (Arnold Delmonico)

Right: Welsh coal for industry from the mining town of Tredegar. Private First Class Herb Heichelbech on leave, looks at 'a dinky little coal wagon' in Colchester's St Botolph's goods yard, September 1944. The rusty wheels and dilapidated state of the adjacent cattle truck show the neglect railway maintenance suffered during the war years. (Robert Sand)

Left: The British complained that it was hard to find an empty taxi when the Yanks were around. A US sailor and a GI de-cab at Kings Cross Station. The Austin is typical of the early 1930s London cabs, with a bulbous horn on the windscreen framing. (Cal Sloan. Airman Memorial Museum)

Right: A train from East Anglia arrives at Liverpool Street Station, London on 13 July 1945. The station received bomb damage in both world wars. (Robert Sand)

Top right: Crossing keeper David Smith on the Shepreth crossing of the Cambridge to London (King's Cross) line. A tedious 24-hour a day task. David lost an arm in a goods railyard accident and was given the crossing keeper's job until he retired. (Cal Sloan)

Right: A Standard saloon at a railway crossing – the gates are being opened – in west Suffolk, 1944. Car owners with essential duties were allowed to run their vehicles with a limited petrol allowance through an issue of coupons. (Mark Brown)

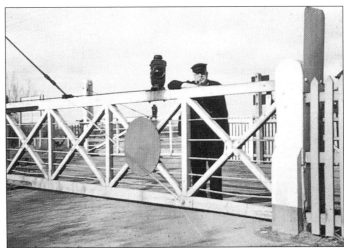

Left: There was nothing like the MG Midget in the States and this popular British sports car was always of interest. Sergeant Gido Turner spotted this one outside a house south of Oxford. Telegraph poles were a permanent feature of all major roadsides but would disappear, although very gradually, after the war. (Robert Astrella)

Right: The double-decker bus was rare outside Britain. Boarding a No. 17, of the Western National for St Ives outside the Beachfield Hotel, Penzance, on an autumn day in 1943. (Robert Astrella)

Below near right: As there was no petrol for private motoring, horsepower came into its own again. A pony and trap near Baldock, Hertfordshire, while a GI pushes his bike up the slope. (Cal Sloan)

Below: The sail barge *Ready* on the River Colne at Marriage's Mill, Colchester, December 1944. This and similar vessels delivered North American grain from the London Docks and ran the risk of being attacked by enemy aircraft while sailing up the east coast. *Ready* survived to be re-named *Mirosa* after retirement and used for pleasure sailing. (Robert Sand)

Right: A laden spritsail barge belonging to F. T. Everard and Sons, of Greenhithe, under way in the Thames. She is towing her boat which, when at sea, would be hoisted in the davits on the starboard quarter. The barges traded anywhere between the Humber and the Solent, and the larger barges went even farther afield. This one is probably the *Lady Mary,* which was built at Greenhithe at the turn of the century. (Cal Sloan)

Left: The spritsail barge *May,* of Ipswich, built in 1891 and owned for many years by Cranfield Brothers, the millers. Throughout the war she took regular cargoes of grain from London Docks to the Ipswich mills. When photographed at anchor in the tideway by a Thames wharf, the skipper had his wife with him. Many barges were destroyed by mines, but *May* survived and was still afloat 50 years on, having achieved considerable success in the various barge races. (Cal Sloan)

Right: The river tug *Wasp* off Gun Wharf, Wapping, with a tow of lighters. This little tug, which belonged to Gaselee & Son Ltd, a well-known firm on the London River, was built of iron at Blackwall in 1890. In peacetime her funnel bore the firm's colours of yellow with red bands, but this was over-painted with grey in wartime. Although a working craft, the pride of her crew is evident through the glistening brasswork. (Cal Sloan)

Below: Scottish west coast lochs were a haven for shipping as they would be less likely to be troubled by enemy aircraft. A coaster loading cargo from a merchant steamer in Loch Fyne. The device over the bows of the larger ship was a protection against acoustic mines. When lowered to the surface of the water a pneumatic drill operating on a steel diaphragm sent out sound waves which would set off the mines well ahead of the vessel. (Cal Sloan)

WAR'S PRESENCE

As the foregoing photographs reveal, the stamp of war was discernible on many seemingly peaceful scenes in the early nineteen-forties. There were more forceful reminders, particularly from the sky. The photographing of military hardware and installations was a punishable offence for all but officially accredited photographers and even then their work had to go before a censor. Although supposedly taboo, the use of personal cameras by US servicemen and women on their own stations was usually subject to a 'blind eye' by the authorities, provided that nothing of a truly secret nature was involved or that camera wielding was not carried out too brazenly. It was fortunate that there were those who were prepared to venture into this realm, otherwise the colour record of extraordinary sights would be sparse indeed and, in many cases, unavailable. Little 'official' colour was turned in this direction.

Left: Four miles above the earth a formation of Fortresses prepares to go to war, their passage marked by the condensation trails caused by hot engine gases in the humid and frigid air. (Cal Sloan)

Below: Turnips flourish on one side of the barbed wire while the adjacent field has sprouted a military camp, Site 6 Barracks at Mount Farm airfield. This land at Drayton St Leonard, Oxfordshire, was no stranger to the foreign soldier, the land between the white posts and the barbed wire marking an ancient road where Roman legions had marched 2,000 years before. (Robert Astrella)

Right: A Norfolk pasture became a woodyard for Attlebridge airbase. Carpentry took the place of cows. (George Parker)

Left: Fortresses coming in to land at Eye, Suffolk after a mission to Germany. (Arnold Delmonico)

Left: The contrails of formations intertwine as hundreds of bombers forge through the icy atmosphere five miles above the earth on their way to strike a target on the Continent. (Robert Sand)